Dedication: TO FRANK, WHOM I MOURN

The Shape of Grief

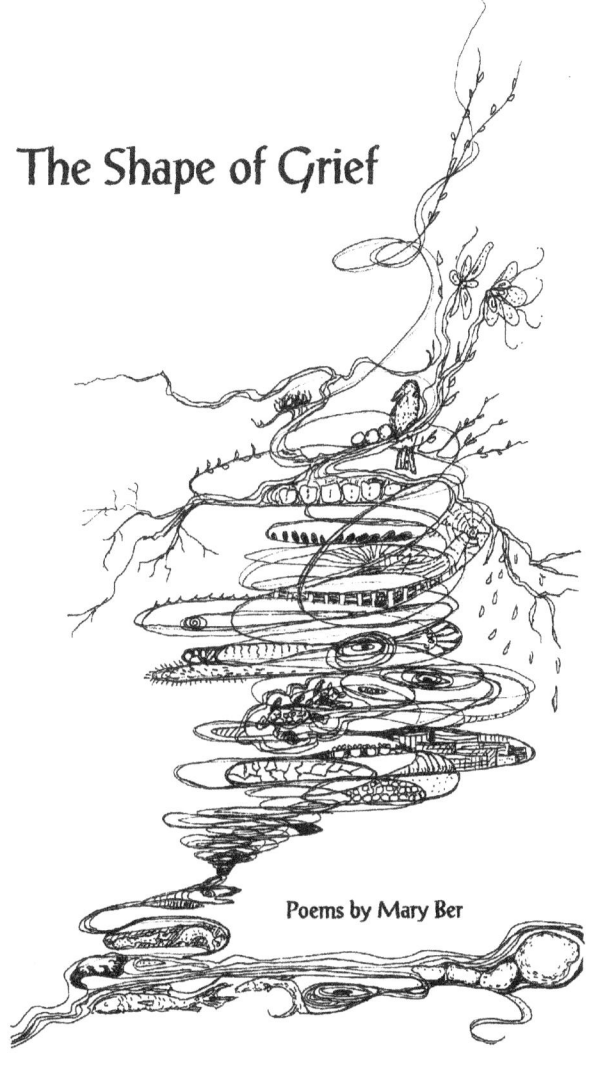

Poems by Mary Ber

Cover design: Lynne Burgess

Prologue: On Defining Widowhood

Remember the time you moved out of one home
    into another:
out of one set of friends
that fit your moments
    and your moods
    and your stories
        into another,
out of one set of shops
and doctors
and weathers
    into another.
Widowhood is like that.
It moves you around
    inside yourself.

You feel like a plant torn loose with all its
    root filaments screaming,
like a swimmer surfacing
    to find the shore in fog.

        ~ ~ ~

You become obsessed with little things

    itching between your toes, numbness in your index finger, a burning eczema on your chin,

    mailing a letter Tuesday, banking a check for $20.00, digging out part of the rosebush that's gone wild

    because

whole more chunks of your life may drop out All your toes and roses Money float away when who knows how much you'll be needing

~ ~ ~

Perhaps the house is too big. Your soul's the size of a pea now. And grief as great as the world. Echoes turn the small rooms into caverns. Grief waits outside like a mean wind and you know you'll carry it with you to the next place like your own breath.

~ ~ ~

*They say
rivers run beneath the earth.
This could be true:
red rivers run under my skin.
I think there must be rivers beneath the soul
and my attention wanders
because
that's where I'm looking for him.*

Preface

    One dark morning about a month after my husband died, I started to make myself breakfast. Poured a cup of coffee, popped some bread into the toaster, took the butter dish out of the fridge. In my usual zombie-like deadness, I waited for the toast to rise. Suddenly I felt zonked; my mind convulsed, and my body bent at the waist. Instinctively I grabbed for a pencil and some of the notepaper that is always handy near the phone.

    Ten poems poured out of me, the first ten poems of this cycle. Poured out so fast I could not keep up with the words. Poured out so insistently that I could not take time to butter the warm and waiting toast. When the poems were finished, I felt like I had watched the ice begin to break on Lake Michigan at the end of winter. Or perhaps like I had coughed up some bread that had lodged in my throat and threatened to choke me. I knew that some kind of inner paralysis had ended; there would be more poems. And they would take me through the journey that is grief.

    They did more than that. They showed me the shape of grief: down and then up, down and up again. And again. But I discovered that traveling through heavy grief is more than a mere cycle journey; it has a spiral shape. It widens one's perception of all reality even as it increases one's compassion for all suffering.

    It is helpful to know the shape of the path one walks. Grieving friends have found some solace in reading these poems, perhaps some of the same solace I found in writing them. Everyone's timetable is different. It took me over two years to complete these poems. Since then, they continue to sing in my heart, a part of the rhythm of my life. I am happy to bring out this second edition in my husband's memory twenty years after his death.

    I've honored the spiral shape of the cycle as it was written, though I've also rearranged some of the poems. (Conscious creating has always been good for art.) And I've structured the cycle around the seasons because they support the shape of grief. My husband died in winter, so I've started there.

THE FIRST WINTER

1

We die of ourselves:
      Old Aunt keels over of slavery;
      Old Uncle rusts away like his stalled car.

Dear Love,
      you rubbed your fingers away last summer;
      you pulled
            your shoulders from their sockets:
            you   would   move   rocks.

And I—
      I watched you from my window,
      stuffed
      myself with books and chocolate,
      watched you garden dill and parsley.

Belly burning,
someday
I shall eat myself to death.

2

When Grandma Pasqual died
my cousin Nick—
a man I barely know—
sent me her picture in a plastic frame.

Conveniently
I substituted us—
our wedding picture.

Smiles open,
we were ready for the cake.

You stand there now,
before me
framed by Death.

How smart of Nick to know
that plastic's best—
much warmer on the lips
than glass.

3

When I came courting you,
a rainbow fish,
I floated poems out to you like seaweed.

They brushed a thousand frondy lips
against you, kissed, whispered my name,
and asked,
"Where are you, Love?
In what dark hole
with amber fish or gold?"

I ask the same tonight:
"Where are you, Love?"
Who made this clear and killing shine
that burns my gills and flings me back
when I leap into it?

I am all curved and scaley question now.
"Where are you, Love?"
I fear this substance
holy fish
call air.

4

It was bad enough
I had Sam take away your winter jackets
so the mouth of the closet
howled like my empty soul.

Why did I spend yesterday's
few hours of sunshine
in your office
sorting,
stripping it?

I can never put them back—
       the papers stuffed in cubbyholes,
       the bags of leather scraps,
       the cracked globe.

I ate the sack of chocolate
       you were saving for the grandkids.
I sold the bag of silver coins
       you hid against thieves.

I went crazy with my cleaning.
Then
night stopped me.

One last drawer
still holds your
years' accumulations.
I will never touch it. Never.

5

Why am I not surprised
poems flow out smooth as molten lava,
perfect laps of grief.

All fire,
pressure at the heart,
creates.

6

I wasn't laughing
when you came in a dream last week
and asked me,
"What's so funny?"
But I'll tell you anyway:

Finding Sue's memorial card
between donations to the Jewish Federation,
how she had your name inscribed
on a brick used in rebuilding
the London theater of Shakespeare,
whom you hated.

Being instructed by that bored city worker
to "Send a death certificate"
so they could excuse you
from your duty as a juror.

Hearing the lady at the cemetery
suggest I buy you a stone that matches Sarah's.
"No"—my weary answer. "No.
A plain stone only. Sarah
was his first wife."

7

Since you made no will
I ask your children
to choose some precious thing
to take from me.

The eldest wants the picture of Jerusalem—
    the most aesthetic, most expensive item.

Another will take
    the leather-sewing Singer he remembers
    Dad treadling through his childhood.
    Up three flights of stairs he'll lug it, set it
    next to antiques he admires
    but cannot use.

A third requests his father's brand new bike,
    a Schwinn dream purchased sixty years too late.
    He'll make one joyous ride
    until it bends,
    much too fragile
    for his heavy need.

A daughter asks
    his sleeping, dreaming chair
    and, safely, she
    will sit young years away.

The youngest wants nothing.
Out of my own
nothingness,
I give it.

8

Grief,
not water,
is the world's most common element.
It pounds down like a shower in the morning.
You swim there all day long
and afterward
sink through it
into night.

Grief is the very air
you gasp
running nowhere.
It burns your throat,
scalds its way down through your blood
singes your heart.

Grief is a faded blanket
you curl yourself around
in secret
like a six-year-old
fearful of the hollow it could leave.
Once
it covered your love
and circled the holy darkness
during nights when his body
pushed back the dome of the sky.

THE FIRST SPRING

9

Today I pasted pictures of our life together
into thick albums,
made a neat stack
of heartbeats.

You would have loved
them. Why
didn't I
do it years ago?

Why didn't you do it yourself!
You always waited
for me to hang up your clothes,
scrub out the sinks,
put both of our lives in order.
Then you'd come
with damp shirts, dirty glasses—
swirl us out
again to chaos.

Now
dark questions burn:
why do I need that chaos? Why
did you let it take you
in the end?

10

Lips that tasted lemon cake and red wine
with you on Pesach mornings after
love under cotton sheets

—my lips—

proclaim,
"Hosanna to the plastic
that covers you!"
Much warmer on the lips than glass
over a photo face,

warmer than the film of ice
over buried earth.

11

You used to drive the yellow school bus up
on schedule,
park for breakfast,
leave a kiss if I was lucky.
Then you'd go again,
and freedom lit my hours like the sun.

Now we're both unscheduled—
you and I.
But suddenly,
warm enough to touch and taste,
you move in my eyes
behind a wall of water.

Then you recede.
I step into relief—
emptiness that is cool
and heartless as shadow,
heavy as truth.

12

This
is a new stage:
you
fading away from me down a sunlit road.
I,
alone in the shadows,
knowing myself
    the ground from which you pull your web of roots,
    the sod around the gaping hole you leave.

Oh, Lover,
you have not been washed,
laid soft in earth.

I am earth.
And I know.

13

Rain
drops
straight
down
among the small, green leaves.

And apple blossoms
perch pink,
shake sweetly
in the brief impact.

Seven years ago
you planted the tree
outside your office window
so you could lift your head
above investments and accounts
to see it bloom
and fruit.

Three month ago
you died.
Now birds poise
their bodies in its branches.
I rest here
a moment—
my eyes
my heart,
my life
white as blossoms.

Rain
deepens the colors:
browns the weathered fence,
shimmers the yellow-green of apple bark.
It glistens leaves.
It sharpens pain.

14

Young apple tree,
our gardener has gone.
I stayed to see your tiny ear-shaped leaves,
your tight, pink buds.

I am here now,
eyes quivering,
hands stroking your bark,
soul caught up among your blossoms, but
heart tangled in
some other sod.

We planted you—
Adam and Eve—
that first warm spring,
then waited several seasons,
harvested
one apple last October,
which we split
and ate.

How sweet
the taste
then.
And this spring,
how bitter
the knowledge.

15

You
start
with a sudden image:
apple trees in bloom,
pink and white enough
to make eyes sting.

You
add
the pang of buying
only one
sweet potato in the grocery store
and passing up
sardines,
a staple over twenty years
of shared lunches.

Now
you are accompanied by
a ghost.

It may leave;
then trees and sweet potatoes
become themselves.

Or you may find
your tongue repeating magic words,
ghostly intonations of
yourself possessed.

16

Grief:
call it
a block of paper
scrolling into your computer's Delphic maw.
It will emerge
and emerge and emerge,
a stream interminable as Styx,
moving, murmuring by itself
long after fingers have left to
cook a chop for dinner.

Call it
a hydra made of water
surging up
through any body opening—
stunned eyes,
hot breath,
bursting bowel.
It's a beast
rising within you,
a monster spilling suddenly
over any moment's peace.

THE FIRST SUMMER

17

Spring rains make swamps
(and so do tears):
murky, sticky traps for careless
moments.

Afterwards in summer gardens,
living roots
tangle together;
tender shoots
pierce the sky.

No so
here;
raw rage
has washed away my humus.

Underneath
I am bedrock—hard, thick granite—
yearning for you
dryly,
soundlessly, always.

18

"Nothing lives forever,"
you always said;
and to prove it,
you died.

You were a whirlwind
in life.
My solid, steady steps
could never keep up,
but you would double back,
take my hand,
fill me with your own lightness.
You made mistakes
surging through life
like that.
Remember when we built our home,
rooted it with fruit trees--and the birch
you carried, on a lark, from north Wisconsin.
Well,
the slim, white birch is dying—
too far south.
The peach trees and the cherry—
too far north—
bleed sap and bow their leaves.

Only
in myself
your roots remain
as Death whirls round and round my thoughts,
a raven
in the orchard.

19

I've read about desert flowers
that open only at night,
teasing, seducing.

Grief can be like that:
a moonflower cactus
heavily calling your
numbed senses
back through the night,
calling your feelings
back to itself,
alive with the fragrance of death
behind desert thorns.

20

This year
all the apples
fall early:
little globes of grief
bordered into countries
by the thin trails of worms.

I slice one open.
Its geography
has burrowed to the core,
veined its milky sweetness
with brown decay.

I throw it back
yet feel myself
hover,
circle above it
like one of the wasps.

21

The birch tree that you lugged
like all your childhood memories,
into alien weather
dies.

Next year I'll plant a poplar:
talking tree,
poet's tree.

22

Grief was a tunnel
I ate myself through.
Now I'm coming out
a bloated slug.
I need new clothes.

Two weeks ago
I bought imported sandals,
a black dress that ripples with colors
as I walk.

Today I sang
that old sixties favorite
we used to harmonize together
in the front seat of the car
while the kids in back
giggled.

People say I'm looking good.
Maybe it's true.
Options unroll before me like magic carpets.
All of them shine.

23

You sit in my mouth now
like a piece of peppermint.
Thoughts of you melt across my tongue
cleansing and moistening dry lips,
leaving sweetness
along with the sting.

THE FIRST AUTUMN

24

Under the ground of my being
tunnels intersect and web.
My strength seeps into darkness
where a silent mole
keeps burrowing,
and things disappear in the tunnels:
invitations, letters,
unshed tears.

I lost a finger
yesterday—
reached down there
for a hidden dream, and
something bit it off.

I walk the surface,
stumble over little hills
asking:
if I cave the tunnels in
what then?
What abut all the lost things?
And what of the mole?
Should I try to trap it
drown it, poison it?

I shudder.
Friends have suggested
recently
I am the mole.

25

At the end of the day,
at the end of the tasks and the business,
at the end of the forest pathway
is the pool.

It can no longer be forgotten
or denied
or avoided.

At the end of the forest pathway
is the pool.
See, it glitters.
It is bottomless.

And round.
Shadowed north to south by trees.
Shadowed east to west by trees.
It is bottomless,
and the path
stops here.

You are alone,
then,
at the end of the path in the forest,
standing before the pool
and the pool is bottomless.

It is made of tears.
It calls your tears.

26 Inanna to Ninshubur*

Eyes sealed,
I sorted my dreams,
fingered tarot cards like braille,
delving desperately
for an river
that would make my grief immortal.

So I came to a sacred city
shut behind seven walls,
and I could see the path I'd walked
slick as snail slime
behind me,
when I passed
through the first wall,
built by Frenzy with a thousand doors;

then the second—
trickier,
fashioned of paneled Mirrors,
unshed tears.

Dizzy with terror
I stumbled into a third wall,
Languor,
crawled through its low door, cheek
scraping dirt.

---

* According to Sumerian mythology, Inanna, the Goddess of Love and Queen of heaven went down to the underworld to visit her sister Ereshkigal, who reigned there. Innanna had to pass through seven gates, at each of which she was divested of a symbol of her royalty. At the end, her sister killed her and hung her rotting corpse on a hook. However, Inanna's vizier, Ninshubur, had been instructed to go for help if the goddess failed to return. She did so, and Inanna was brought back to life.

I did not rise at the fourth wall.
Welcoming Sickness
opened its rainbow door at my advance:
bruise-blue,
fever-red,
yellow-green with poison,
it swung
on hinges oiled for silence.

So I rested,
vacant,
grateful, no more effort needed—
a spent caterpillar
on a broken branch
drifting with humid winds
to the fifth door, Death.

I must have entered all unknowing.

Once inside,
dull surges
slowly pushed my shell
and I emerged—no butterfly—a wasp
equipped to sail across the sixth wall,
Spite,
but not before a practice sting or two.

And so to the seventh wall—
the white-hot wall of Anger,
where my demon self
waits on the ramparts shifting shapes:
lock for my key,
cup for my blood.

Do not go bathing in the pool by moon-light.
I will rise before you,
a crocodile,
and measure you with my jaws.

Do not go apple-picking
in the sunlight.
At the base of trees
I coil myself
with forked tongue
testing air.

You cannot know me now,
and I feel your image
fade from my mind like smoke into winter sky.

I have nothing to give you now but this bitter warning
kissed by my fingers
the last to remember love.

~ ~ ~

But if I am not come again in three days,
come again my Self—
if I am not come—

lose no time, Friend!
Cry out to the dancing goddesses.
Lose no time;
cry
gold tears to the singing gods.

WINTER AGAIN

27

I dined with Ereshkigal*.
We had red
tea, bone-white cakes. Then she had
me.

I was ground up,
made liquid,
passed through all her pulsing
tunnels,
through the holy
throne.

"I shall know,"
I said,
"dark peace
or shining birth again."
"Not so," she laughed.

Under the throne
I found
Darkness
vast as the unfolding cosmos—
and creatures
even Ereshkigal
cannot name.

* See note for Poem 26

28

Do the slugs have a queen?
If so,
call me Slug Queen:
living in a slimy cavern,
fed slug jelly by a thousand sightless slaves,
excreting thoughts like eggs
(unfertilized, ungendered)
all the while fattening,
fattening
like a monstrous tuber in the earth.

29

"The lake at last,"
I always think,
slipping down beneath its waters,
having earned the right to sleep.

Sounds
wash away like dust,
I feel my closed eyes brush
against dreams all finned and frondy,
and the shadow of a Dolphin
on deepest blue-green throne.

Then rise refreshed---
morning like a shore,
sky white with gulls and egrets,
pilings
(dead and gray last night)
blooming into pelicans.

Under sun
pouring through the winter skylights
wooden tables in my living room
creak.
Is it a cry—
old wood remembering how sap sighed
up living roots
and laughed into cool, green leaves?
Is it
the synchronous
movement of wood spirits
touched by some passing energy
I cannot see,
a restless stirring of trapped souls, warmed
and waiting the Final Judgment of the trees?

I only know it is a holy sound
that calls for repentance
and a new heart.

Since I do not answer
I can hear crystals chatter
softly in the cabinet,
chatter and chide.

31

Now if I take to my skin again—
I give no promises—
but if I stretch
that cracked case back
over dreams and breathing,
if I soak my dried cells
in the brown Euphrates,
if I pull muscles
gone rigid as wires
gently over the raw bone joints—

will I have strength enough to take
the first next step
and then the next
first step?

I have always loved
pictures that call me into journeys,
promising song and wind
and fragrant salt beyond the frames:

star-guided seas
with Yankee clippers cutting east
perhaps to diamond-white South Africa,

and sunlit glades
half-ringed with brooding trees,
one brown path pointing
west,

up-curving roads
that promise wondrous valleys just beyond
the bulging hill.

Plain country scenes
and simple photographs
caught by some soul
who knows that paths are promises
and frames
the guide to faith.

33   **Isis***

I mourn Osiris—
he who made the sun
to set and rise again.

I come before
the scales of judgment towards the end
of this oppressive journey
balancing
the salt tears in my soul
with the stones in my heart—
and the stones are not heavy enough—
measuring
all the grief in my tears
by shadows cast from stars—
and the shadows are not long enough.

Time alone
can turn the balance—
Time
sitting on the stones
one blessed moment more:

until the scale pan rises
to the level of the eyes
and the tears pour out
and stones
rest gently on the thirsty grasses
and the day star burns
bright and joyous in the morning air.

---

* Isis is the Egyptian goddess who, after her consort Osiris was murdered by his brother, sailed the world retrieving parts of his mutilated body and then brought him back to life.

SPRING AGAIN

34

From behind
glass patio doors,
my varnished tables
watch board fences
colored green with moss,
alive in
cold rain.

35

Snow whitens the jonquils.
I spend this morning on the phone, disconnected:
hours on hold
with generic muzak,
and the senseless rituals programmed
by robots of technology.

Then I sleep from twelve to three,
(the crucifixion hours),
wake relieved—
Good Friday over
and the lemon cake of Pesach
eaten
years ago.

36

We planted pussy willow in the
wrong place:
fruit trees block it during summer months.
But I can see it now
behind the stiff, dark cherry—
silver supple arms
catching whatever spring bleak April offers—

and I need no other
Easter flowers.

37   Inanna to Ninshubur*

I am writing this to tell you
I have found
the river underground—
the one that feeds into my lake.

And since I've vowed to track it
hard, hard against the current
like a salmon over rapids
over smooth sand, sharp gravel,
deep pools of peace;
track it through its thrilling coldness,
through great caverns, narrow tunnels,
track it to the mouth of darkness,
its fierce and vital source—

I am writing this to tell you
it will be awhile
before I write again.

*See note to poem 26

SUMMER AGAIN

38

I have risen at dawn to birdsong,
sent blue life
through a long, green hose to the roses,
said a sharp thing to my neighbor
and a true thing to my daughter,
thought the afternoon away on friends
as I cleaned
brown kitchen shelves.

Now in the dark of the moon I see
moments of our time together
set against black leaves of loss
like sunny living photos—
sweet,
complete.

39

I thought the Rand McNally globe was seamless
'til it cracked
when I dropped it—
circled open like an old oatmeal carton
(bare inside, gray and empty),
like two orange halves with segments
lifted out,
like a bright December dreidel
split in two.

Free of all the central mystery,
now its rivers flow in pencil,
and its mountains clot in paste,
its meridians imposed
by sheer imagination.

I fitted it together,
every lake, ocean, continent—
no scratches, tears or gouges,
just awareness of the seam
and the shadow of Persephone
that vanished in the sun.

Then I thought of the moment,
I remembered the instant
when Death cracked you open
and your spirit flew like darkness from the core.

40

On my property,
in the circle of my domesticity,
where, before we knew better,
we planted the grapevine
that doesn't belong there—
you robins settled in

I tried to poke your nest out
as I had in spring.

Perched in the gutter, twigs in your beak,
you glared in anger,
launched your shrill
protest
from the neighbor's fence,
the plum tree and
rose trellises.

"OK! OK!"
I threw my pole down in disgust.
"OK, you win!"
And so I watched
you beat me to the berry bush each morning.
A tenant now,
you really had the right.

I also learned
a little of your language:
shrieks
each time I roamed my patio,
raw rage
if I should near the nest,
most dewy mornings and late afternoons
a cheerful chirp
assuring all was well.

Then yesterday, a different sound:
the high, demanding cries
that signal hungry children everywhere.
"Hah! Serves you right," I murmured,
looking up between
the covers of my book.
But when I went
to pick my berries,
silence hovered, like
dust in the noon sun,
over the specks of insects
darting around
the still and awkward bones
of the white-bellied fledgling
underneath the plum.

You hadn't a thing to say,
perched in the tree
a few scant feet away.
And later still
a bush away
you went on with your harvesting
as I did mine.

But how you followed me
protesting as,
a little later on,
I bore the fledgling to the evergreens
on shovel tip,
and in a shallow hole,
I buried the child.

Peace, bird,
I know about death:
the moment when,
too weak to move the dirt,
you watch another
shovel it over the darling of your heart.

I know what it means
to stand outside the circle
silent and waiting
while the love of your life
star-wanders in the cosmos of his father
or sleeps
in his mother's arms.

Again, bird,
peace!
Let us lift our throats
in the green of summer
and pray each bit of earth become
black hope.
Let us join in duet,
sing salvation to each other.

Friend,
we are all out of place;
we are all at home.

41

I dreamed I saw sea turtles
fly over a clearing
where I waited for you—
and life was risky
but green.

Awake now,
I pray for the courage
to rise like the turtles
despite my heavy
flesh,
and thick layers of living—
complete the pattern,
lift,
and circle home

42

The moist summer night,
a waterfall of darkness,
slides over the skin of my soul.
Life dwells in the darkness
like the water I cannot see.
And it knows me.
And it holds me.

43

Sometimes
the thought of you,
of all you said and did and were,
seeps into me like butter into warm bread,
lies calmly on me like
September sun.

AUTUMN AGAIN

44 Poem on Our Wedding Anniversary

Last year
shock stunned me into sleeping,
and I dreamed my way from autumn
straight through spring.

This year
pain
pricks me into knowing.
And I hate this swollen-berried,
dusty-golden,
sunlight-speckled fall.

It will brittle away
like grapevine tendrils,
blow away like powdered mildew,
slime away in autumn showers like rain-plastered leaves.
And its days will grey into November,
thicken into slushy slowness,
harden into death.
A smoky wind
blows winter's promise
now.

Like all who hear it
rattle blood-red leaves,
I wait
in hate.

45

When I was alive
in this tide pool,
I learned everything the waves washed in.
Each low tide left me fatter,
shining. . .filled.

Now I am dead;
the tide pool is between-land;
knowledge that crests,
breaks full and foamy,
drenches me with truth,

rolls out again in low tide,
leaving me empty,
the tongue of my soul licking
my own dry shell.

46

Constipated,
holding tears hard
in hidden tunnels,
my soul squats.

THE THIRD WINTER

47

Sixty Minutes
had a special
on the live
deadly
sarcophagus at Chernobyl:
how the grave keepers
shroud themselves,
race through tunnels,
lest the breath
of the Monster
rest too long
on their futures.

I have built such a structure
over grief.
It looks harmless
on the landscape,
but I tend it,
terror-stricken,
shroud myself
for quick inspections of the dials,
knowing white-hot, primal matter
could spirit into poison
any minute
during the next
ten thousand years
of my life.

48   Inanna's* Second Journey

The truth is
I am called by Ereshkigal,
dragged screaming by the demons
with my lover Dumuzi.

And the darkness at the nearest gate
is awful as they tear our hands apart,
for I know Black Ereshkigal is
waiting open-mouthed and hungry
at the core.
I can hear my lover waiting
as they pass him like a flower
hand by hand
to the mouth of Ereshkigal
where the air is hot with hunger
and the dark is thick with teeth.

At the second gate I swell
like a slug,
crack my crown and shining bracelets,
split my cloak and supple sandals,
strain against my very skin,
for the call of Ereshkigal
draws my spirit from its sockets,
pulls my very soul against me,
and I fester with the effort
to breathe.

At the third gate I grow quiet,
still enough to hear the footsteps
of my viceroy Ninshubur
as she flees.
Though her quick feet speed in silence,
grains of sand against the shadow
signal flight.

And part of me cries, "Traitor!"
but my rod of justice trembles
to remind me that Ninshubur
heard no calling to this journey.
Strong and beautiful Ninshubur
has the right to stream and sun.
Four more awful gates await me
as I walk toward Ereshkigal,
and the very demons cower
slinking backward into darkness
from the maw.
So I move toward Ereshkigal
who has called me to this meeting,
to this second journey's union.

Ah, they tell me she is sister,
but I feel a deeper secret:

beating in the inner darkness
under gates of skin and sinew,
back of portals arched in ivory,
my heart knows its own self.

---

* According to Sumerian mythology, Inanna, the Goddess of Love and Queen of heaven went down to the underworld to visit her sister Ereshkigal, who reigned there. Innanna had to pass through seven gates, at each of which she was divested of a symbol of her royalty. At the end, her sister killed her and hung her rotting corpse on a hook. However, Inanna's vizier, Ninshubur, had been instructed to go for help if the goddess failed to return. She did so, and Inanna was brought back to life.

49

Like a fragile bit of celery leaf
on top of unskimmed soup,
I balance on each minute
feeling
the fire beneath
and bones boiling.

50

Oh my Dear, I have
given you back to the stars.
What more can they ask?

51

In Israel we looked at mountains,
strained against the heated haze,
your hand on my shoulder—
always on my shoulder—
sinking through the white film of my blouse
like desert sun.

I can still feel it
sometimes
on my shoulder squared for conflict
on my shoulder bent for burdens,
on my shoulder curved for sleep.

52

Figure in the mirror—
    curious Beauty
    soon to sleep for seeking knowledge;
    brave Arachne challenging the gods;
    bright Ariadne leading Love to safety;
    shrewd Penelope, weaver of shining shrouds;
    Grandmother Spider, old and great with stories—
give me silk
filaments for picture-making,
strong
threads to loop
beneath my sinking feet.

THE THIRD SPRING

53

The house we built was mostly filled with us,
and in the night,
we curtained off our dreams,
snuffed out our light,
sure-footed in a darkness thick with love.

But when you died, bleak Emptiness arrived,
left His signature on every dust mote,
brooded in the shadows of each chair.

Alarmed,
I lit the vacant rooms at evening—
let them blaze
brilliant
'til the scalding sun.

Last night Shame
defeated Cowardice,
turned out the bulbs,
pulled back the curtain,
and the kindly Moon
called "Sister" to a round hope in my soul,
kept vigil 'til the daystar rose again
while I slept in light.

54

I always wanted to be married
under a canopy of flowers.
We were wed
by a Justice of the Peace
in City Hall.
I have my blossoms now.
Magnolias are magnificent this year.
I see them from a distance—huge
undulating cups of springtime.
Then I saunter toward the foamy,
fluted trees that line this pebbled path.
Mating ducks and sparrows
make an anthem
as I walk this aisle
under branches vaulted like a
pink and white cathedral.
But blooms are past their prime.
I feel
yesterday's fallen petals
under foot, while
overhead
flowers edged in brittle brown
flutter wearily;
the sky between
soaks up gray from earth
as sunlight fades.
I see your face, my dear,
and white
petals shaped like teardrops
float around me.
I send them all to you—
wherever you are.

55 On My Birthday

Today I feel ready for ravens:
      When I die
          Bleach my bones in sun;
          Soak them in salt sea,
thrust
them deep into sulfurous earth.
Clean me.
Clean me.

THE THIRD SUMMER

56

There are nights
I pray for dreams
where spirits
shoot across the sky
like comets

and nights
I just want to hear
rain on the roof
just hard hard rain on the roof
just rain
rain. . .

57

Here
in this blessed moment,
peaceful as a beach
when the waves of pain recede,
I pause before my next breath,
adjusting rhythm
to the beat I feel so surely all around.

Between each breath and heartbeat
lies the tunnel to eternity.
My toes have touched it.

How can I not believe
the stars are dancing!

58

Let me die
heavy as an August raindrop
falling of its own fullness.

EPILOGUE

*We can know the future
if we know the past:
it cycles . . .*

*A visitor in Amsterdam,
a member of a tourist group,
I watched my students
stumble down the bus steps to a door
of an item on the day's itinerary.*

*A little past the entrance
I locked eyes with a painted girl
held prisoner in the Rijksmuseum
corridor,
and was swept beyond her
by the stream of tourists
flowing toward a Rembrandt,
and then rushed to buses
that emptied in Vienna.*

*How she haunted me,
her brown dress blending with the window shadows,
sunlight on her warm cheek
glowing like the peaches
underneath the sill,
her young eyes dreaming
of a husband,
freedom,
future.*

*Years later as I wandered through that city
by your side, my Prince, my Love,
I saw the building beckon in the distance
like a past friend
decades older,
only recognized
by soul-light in the eyes.*

*I rose from the suitcase where I'd slumped,
a weary pilgrim in the noon of travel.
"Let's stow our stuff at some hotel," I said.
"Then take me there."*

*And so you did,
my tale about the girl unwinding
as we threaded through the centuries' cobbled streets.*

*But the quaint castle,
the building pretty-painted at a distance
loomed huge and vast an hour before its closing.
"We'll never find her now," I mourned.
You tightened
your hand in mine.
Lit only by my words you led me straight
down darkened corridors to where she waited,
alone in the light of an empty room.
You sat me on the bench
and said, "Now look
as long as you like.
Mary, that girl was you."*

(Continued)

*It is my prayer to God
and you
that death come like the Rijksmuseum—
a glimpse through narrow passages
with you beside me
leading through
the great gray doorway
and the knowledge
that the lady
has been waiting through the eons
with sweet peaches
in her hand.*

Wedding Anniversary Poem

I remember the way you walked:
compact, erect,
heart low to the ground,
sure-footed despite your limp.

You never bent
your head to ward off stumbles.
You never bent
your neck in the face of the wind.

I closed the last page of the book
I made about you
months of tears ago.
One poem more! Because
it must not be forgotten:
how well you walked the earth.

Acknowledgments

I am very grateful to Jude Rittenhouse, who shared my grief as she offered valuable suggestions to the poems; also to Lynne Hume burgess and Mary Colgan McNamara, whose comments I cherish.

Above all, I am grateful to the friends in the Moon Journal Readouts, who shared my grief as I poured it in poetry month after month, year after year.

I also wish to thank editors of the following publications in which my poems first appeared, sometimes in a slightly different version or title.

Arlington Heights Journal: # 32
Daily Herald: "Prologue: On Defining Widowhood"
Jane's Stories II: # 38, # 40
Moon Journal: # 40
Pudding Magazine: # 44, "Epilogue"
100 Words: #20
When a Lifemate Dies: Stories of Love, Loss, and Healing: # 16, # 18, # 23

Editor: Mary H. Ber
Graphic Design: Phyllis Natanic, Karl Moeller
Consulting Design: Jan Bottiglieri
Production Assistants: Helen Quade, Ishwara Thomas

Second Edition
Copyright ©Mary H. Ber 2015

www.ingramcontent.com/pod-product-compliance
Lightning Source LLC
Chambersburg PA
CBHW072106290426
44110CB00014B/1854